Become
UNSTOPPABLE

Become UNSTOPPABLE

TURN *FEAR* TO *FAITH*. UNLOCK YOUR POTENTIAL AS AN ENTREPRENEUR.

A handbook for entrepreneurs who are ready to stop playing small, and get the clarity and confidence they need to unlock their potential as an entrepreneur.

NATHALIE GUERIN

BECOME UNSTOPPABLE
TURN FEAR TO FAITH. UNLOCK YOUR
POTENTIAL AS AN ENTREPRENEUR.

iUniverse books may be ordered through booksellers or by contacting:

iUniverse
1663 Liberty Drive
Bloomington, IN 47403
www.iuniverse.com
844-349-9409

Because of the dynamic nature of the Internet, any web addresses or links contained in this book may have changed since publication and may no longer be valid. The views expressed in this work are solely those of the author and do not necessarily reflect the views of the publisher, and the publisher hereby disclaims any responsibility for them.

Any people depicted in stock imagery provided by Getty Images are models, and such images are being used for illustrative purposes only. Certain stock imagery © Getty Images.

ISBN: 978-1-6632-2860-4 (sc)
ISBN: 978-1-5320-9437-8 (hc)
ISBN: 978-1-5320-9438-5 (e)

Print information available on the last page.

iUniverse rev. date: 12/14/2021

CONTENTS

Acknowledgements... ix

Introduction... xi

Principle #1: Use Your Divine Connection 1

Principle #2: Believing Is a Choice—Choose It 15

Principle #3: Follow What Energizes You 29

Principle #4: Take the Wheel 49

Principle #5: Practice Alignment 59

About the Author 79

Dedicated to Jeanna Gabellini.

I was lost, and you put me back on my path. Thank you!

ACKNOWLEDGEMENTS

It's important to me to acknowledge a special group of people who have inspired me. Some are family, teachers, coaches, and clients, while others have been mere acquaintances. No matter what category you find yourself in, you can be sure that this book would not have existed without you. To all of you, I say thank you.

This book would not have been possible without Lindsay Fisher, my editor. You not only edited this book but also taught me to be a better writer along the way. The latter is a gift I will never forget. Thank you!

I'd like to say thanks to my family—my parents, Benoits and Jeanine Guerin, as well as Denise, Sylvie, and Eric—for their constant support and encouragement. Also, the following individuals for their friendship, coaching, and teachings: Becky T. Dickson, Jeanna Gabellini, Narayan Joti, Toby Macklin, and Farveh Momayezzadeh. My world is better because of you.

INTRODUCTION

Our deepest fear is not that we are inadequate. Our deepest fear is that we are powerful beyond measure. It is our light, not our darkness that most frightens us. —Marianne Williamson

Do you remember the moment you decided to make a go of your business? I was sitting in an interview for a twelve-month IT contract as a project manager. I was there because my latest contract had been abolished when the budget got slashed by $100 million. I really hadn't planned on that, and I was freaking out about the money. And then two managers across from me asked why I wanted to work there.

I don't want to work here! I thought. *Oh wait. I don't have to be here.*

That was the moment I decided to start my own business. Now, I knew it would be hard, but I didn't know it would be *that* hard. Five months in, I was totally burned out from spending 15 hours a day on Facebook (and probably because

I slept with my phone and checked my newsfeed at three in the morning). Little did I know this was only the beginning of my struggle.

I invested in expensive coaches to show me the path. I did what they told me to do: webinars, Facebook ads, challenges, mindset work, etc. I got lots of leads and got some clients, but it was never enough. It didn't matter if it was a $27 offer or a $6,000 service—with each failure, my confidence went down, and my self-esteem all but disappeared. It left me angry, bitter, and resentful. I'd created a business to make an impact in the world and to be able to travel when I wanted to. I felt trapped in a nightmare.

What was wrong with me? Why is it so hard to get clients?

As the months, days, and years went by, I was obsessed with one question: what am I doing wrong? I know—just asking the question kept me stuck, but I was so deep in a pit of despair I couldn't make my way back to hope.

I opened Messenger one day to find a message from an acquaintance: *You can't doubt yourself!*

I winced at her words. My heart sank, and I couldn't argue with the truth. I'd lost my faith. Worse, I knew I couldn't help anyone in my current state. Heck, *I* wouldn't even hire me. It was no surprise the amazing clients I wanted to work with were running in the other direction. My insecurity was why I was miserable, depressed, and broke.

Every time I thought about quitting and started to look for a job, I would end up "trying one more thing"—a new offer, a new strategy, another email. There's just a part of me that will never give up. My friends call this *resilience*. My doctor calls this *obsessive-compulsive disorder*. Yes, you need a little bit of that energy to succeed as an entrepreneur.

My breakthrough finally came in a vision I had during a meditation. In my vision, I saw myself picking up love and bringing it back into my heart. It was in that moment that I started to love myself. I realized everything I need comes from within. It comes from my spirit. It's not something I have to do; it's something I must allow to come from me. After the spiritual awakening, I stopped being so hard on myself, and I started following what brought me joy. This, by the way, is the art of self-love.

Everything you need to succeed is inside of you.

Choosing to believe in yourself, the universe, and the process is how you become unstoppable as an entrepreneur. It's how you unlock your potential and start making a lot more moola every month. The secret is knowing how to get in alignment—a state where you know the universe has heard your request and is figuring out the best path for you moving forward.

It's a state where no matter how much money you're making, you know there is plenty and that all is well. It's a state where you know you're enough, and you give yourself permission to be in complete alignment with your offers, your content, your marketing, and your sales.

The secret? Reconnect with your inner being and allow your truth, your greatness, out into the world. When you stand in your truth and allow yourself to shine your light in the world, you are the person you were born to be.

Just believe. Trust yourself. You're enough. You've got this.

Entrepreneurial advice is like weight-loss: while there are just as many business strategies as there are diet variations, strategy alone almost always falls flat, because strategy doesn't go far enough inward. It may ease a symptom but doesn't actually cure the disease. It doesn't help you believe in yourself.

Confidence can be challenging, of course, when you face uncertainty. How do you trust yourself when you just don't have a clue what you are supposed to do next?

You're way more than just those thoughts! Your vibration—your strongest emotions—about a desire is the sum of your positive and negative feelings about it.—Margaret Lynch

Telling yourself *I've got this* is pointless if the underlying truth is that you feel unable or inadequate or doomed to failure. You can say the same thing over and over to yourself, but if you don't believe it, it won't be effective. Whatever you believe most is the vibration you send out into the universe.

When I first started my business, I focused on helping entrepreneurs find and remove their limiting beliefs so they could manifest clients. What I found, though, is that the work around deeper, more personal beliefs is what allowed them to step into their purpose. We could talk about hiccups in business and work out one kink, but they'd always be back when the next surfaced, because we never looked at the root cause of the issue (or what kept them reverting to old habits even when they found brief success).

After years of building her vision board but never finding success, one client came to me so she could finally get unstuck in her life and business. In sessions, we'd clear her blocks, and like clockwork, she'd receive unexpected clients afterwards. It was uncanny. But it wasn't until we worked on her beliefs about herself that the deeper transformation happened, so she could finally step into her power to consistently succeed on her own. Once she believed in herself, she was able to finally allow her greatness to expand out into the world.

This book shows you how to do that too. And while I will show you the steps, and suggest and share experiences, nothing is better than the day when you finally realize that you are good enough. You'll know you've got this, and you'll know how to bring yourself back to that powerful energy whenever you slip. The truth is, it's *your* job to believe in *you*.

I'm a little bit embarrassed to tell you, but I didn't learn this lesson until I ran out of money and was forced to stop working with coaches. I was scared, wondering what I'd do without a coach, how I'd make it, and who would believe in me.

I started looking for an IT job and soon found out that wasn't really an option. Not only was my heart not in it, but four years is a long time to be out of the IT project-management world. For the first time in years, I got into alignment and asked myself what I really wanted to do in terms of processes and offers. What would bring me joy?

Then I went out and did it. I chose to believe in myself and in what I really wanted. I chose to put the fear aside and focus on faith. I chose to take another step. In that, I became unstoppable. Six weeks later, I was finally at five-figure months. (And yes, it stayed that way).

The path to unlocking your potential as an entrepreneur

The rest of the book takes you through the five principles of unlocking your potential as an entrepreneur and becoming unstoppable. As you go through them, you'll learn to unleash your greatness and believe in yourself. Of course, you'll also learn how to help the Universe assist you in creating your dream life and business.

You'll discover how to get confident about sales, even if you hate them; clear the noise of the online world, so you can follow your path; deal with the fear of being judged; and keep going when you're unsure of the steps to take. Finally, in the last principle, you'll discover how to keep going even when the shit hits the fan. By the end of this book, you'll know how to manage the emotional roller-coaster that can keep you lost and broke (but only if you let it).

My recommendation is that you go through every step, do the exercises, and see what your experience is like while implementing my strategies. Then, trust your gut. Take what fits and throw out the rest.

No matter how much you doubt your ability or how scared you are of messing everything up, no matter how many times you've been rejected or how many times you stopped yourself from asking for the sale, or even if you've never felt ready or you've been rejected a thousand times: if you're ready to step out from the shadows of your greatness and start creating a purposeful, financially successful business, you can. Yes, even if you've invested buckets of money in gurus and failed so many times you don't believe success is possible anymore.

You are brave, courageous, and resilient enough. You are smart enough. When you choose to believe you have everything you need inside, and you allow yourself to express it, you'll become unstoppable, unlock your potential, and start creating the *life* you were born to live.

Let's go.

Principle #1
Use Your Divine Connection

You are an infinite spiritual being having
a temporary human experience.
—Dr. Wayne Dyer

Being an entrepreneur is a lot like being a superhero. You're born to impact the world. You may not be able to stop bullets or be able to fly, but you are strong, and you have gifts only you can share. Only you can fulfill your life's purpose. Whether you know it or not, it's why you started your business and why you want it to be successful. It's your way of going out into the world and making a difference.

Just like most superheroes and many of my clients, you've been hiding your true self from the world. Maybe you've been told you were too much, and you learned to be different in order to be accepted. Perhaps you're not altogether comfortable being in the spotlight. Somewhere along the way, you started believing something was wrong with you. Maybe you were too quiet, too loud, too nerdy, too rational, too creative, too sensitive, or too popular. You started to believe the lie that what makes you unique is a liability and not an asset.

To make matters worse, you don't think you have any superpowers—you've totally forgotten them. You are out in the world in a version of you that is only a subset of you. You play small; you play to please other people. Like Clark Kent, you've dimmed your light to fit in.

It's time to stop.

You're not average, and you have superpowers the world needs. That's why you were put on this earth. It's why you were born. It's the secret unlocking your potential.

It's true, some people may not be comfortable with you standing in your greatness, sharing your truth, and being the light for others to see. So what? You don't have to pick up their energy and make it your own. You don't have to save them either. You can stand there and be the lighthouse for all to see. When you do this, those who are ready for you will come. Trust me—ready people are out there.

This suppression of your greatness is why there are times when you feel lost, forgotten, and disconnected. It's why you keep running on the hamster wheel chasing something that never comes. It's why you've picked up a book on unlocking your potential. It's why you keep trying to figure out what people want. Doing this long enough leads to depression (I know, I've been there). It takes a massive amount of energy to suppress one's greatness. It also kills your confidence and makes you afraid of playing full-out as an entrepreneur.

Where do your superpowers come from?

I believe there is a universal life force running through all things. It's called God, Source, CHI, Universe, and Infinite Intelligence, just to name a few. As humans, we have a connection to this universal life energy via our spirit, which is sometimes called our inner being or soul. The true source of your power comes from this universal life force. When you stand in your truth fully connected to universal energy, you're not only in alignment but also capable of allowing your superpowers to come through.

There was a time I wanted nothing to do with spirituality. The word *God* made me cringe, and I thought prayer was for the crazy. Even through five years of therapy, I never allowed myself to go down a spiritual path. When a friend of mine gave me a book with the word *God* for my birthday, I never opened it. Then, one day, I realized I was dying for human connection, and I couldn't think of anything else to do, so I went to a spiritual center. Honestly, I just didn't know how else to heal the plaguing pain, emptiness, and depression I felt.

The first time I walked into a spiritual center to attend a spirit circle was a late October night just before Halloween. I didn't know what a spirit circle was. To be honest, I was terrified that ghosts would come out of the walls and scare the crap out of me. Spoiler alert: that didn't happen.

Instead, the medium took us through a guided visualization to help us connect with our spirit guides. Afterwards, she channeled messages for us, receiving information and sharing it with us. She connected to my energy and ask Spirit what I needed to know. One woman in the group got news that her son was doing well in spirit, while another was told that her abundance was coming.

I don't remember what message I received from Spirit that night, but I'll never forget the medium asking if anyone had received their own message from spirit. I looked up at her and thought she was crazy. Me? I'm just a normal person. I work in IT. I'm not sure I even believe in all this spiritual stuff.

Just as I was dismissing it, I heard God's voice in my right ear: "Tell him he's OK, but he doesn't know it yet. Tell him." The message I'd received from God was meant for the man sitting across from me. I shared the message with him.

As unexpected as receiving divine guidance was, it also felt familiar. I realized in that moment that I'd been receiving guidance my whole life, but it was the first time I'd been asked to share. I did.

That night was like being plugged into universal energy. I learned later that this is what happens when you raise your vibration via meditation and allow yourself to reconnect to universal life force. You simply become a channel. In that moment, all the pain you've experienced just goes away.

I got hooked.

This is when I started a daily practice of connecting to universal energy. I started by asking for a new job, and within three months, after years of trying, I finally made the transition into IT consulting. This gave me the time and the energy to finish a book, become a coach, and become a healer

I found unstoppable confidence and momentum, and so can you.

Even if the change is slow at first, the more actions you take, the more change occurs. Eventually, the actions add up, and you find yourself moving faster, just as with anything you practice. It's like trying to ride your bike uphill. The first push is hard, but then, as you keep pushing, it gets easier and you go faster. With your momentum comes a greater connection to Source energy. You give more, and you get more back.

You are a divine human being. It's time for you to use your gift.

You need to know that like you, I'm a human, and I'm not always super-connected. Sometimes, I'm downright mad at God and want nothing to do with anything spiritual.

I spent years in my business trying to push my way to success and found myself going headfirst into massive brick walls because I'd stopped using my connection to source energy. I thought I could "logic" through it, forcing my way through business without my intuitive guides supporting me. Now I know better, and when I don't feel connected to Source, I meditate and regain that connection before making any decision.

Unsure how you'll know you're not connected to divine energy? You'll know when you're feeling off. Maybe you'll feel frustrated your offers aren't selling, angry you're not getting paid what you're worth, or stuck in overthinking and paralysis. The truth is, you'll doubt yourself at every turn. You need to know that's normal; we are human, and it is definitely a human quality to question everything.

However, reconnecting to your truth will allow you to regain your power and belief in yourself despite hardship and worry. It will allow you to live your purpose and expand your light into the world.

If you're struggling to hear and trust your own divine connection, you're not alone. When I first started my business, I put my divine guidance aside and started to follow a brute-force strategy. I spent 12 to 14 hours a day scrolling Facebook feeds. It was fun for a while, and I did get clients, but then I got very tired. I stopped showing up, and the constant stream of clients stopped flowing. Fear set in. Nothing worked to raise my vibe: not meditation, not the 100 gratitude statements I wrote every day, not the healings I was constantly sending myself. I was exhausted, scared, and angry.

Then, one day, I had a tantrum. I yelled at God, "I didn't sign up for this. This is too damn hard. I demand $500 today. I don't care how you do it. Just tell me what you want me to do and I'll do it. Prove to me that it's easy and fun."

Getting those thoughts out of my system felt so good. A few minutes later, I had an idea pop into my head to offer my tribe an intuitive reading to help them raise their vibe. I'd had this idea before and discounted it because it was just too weird, but on that day, I leaned in fully. Why? Because I'm a woman of my word, and I'd just told God I'd do whatever he suggested.

That night, I created a post about my new offer on Facebook. I wasn't attached to the outcome. In fact, I thought it was simply too late in the day to get any traction. An hour later, I'd made $600. It was completely magical. That turned into $12,000 over three weeks.

I knew about the Law of Attraction and what is possible, but it wasn't until I had that experience of making $12,000 over three weeks that I really got it. Getting clients and making money doesn't have to be hard.

It's what possible when you actually get out of your own way and follow your divine guidance.

Jessica's Story

"Why can't it just be easy?"

That's the question Jessica, a mindset coach, asked during a coaching call. She was frustrated that the launch to sell a course had resulted in only one sale. This despite the fact that she'd invested time, energy, and money in doing everything right.

I didn't miss a beat and told her that it could be easy, but first she would need to release this idea that launching and selling had to be hard and accept that it could indeed be easy by taking divine inspired action. She was on board with the idea but was also skeptical. We spent the rest of our call releasing resistance.

At the end of our time together, I asked her what would be fun and easy. She checked in with her divine guidance and immediately said she'd like to be a guest on a podcast and lead free hot-seat coaching workshops. Even though there was no clear plan of how this was going to lead to clients, she decided to follow the path because it felt good.

Five minutes after our call ended, she booked herself a podcast interview. That podcast interview turned into a free workshop, which led to enrolling five people into her course.

"I can't believe how easy it was," she told me.

How do you tap into and use your divine connection?

A lot of people think they should always follow their gut like it's never wrong. I say check in with yourself and see where the information is coming from. If it's coming from fear or lack, following it will keep you stuck. Well, unless you're being chased by a giant tiger.

Your brain can't tell the difference between real fears and imaginary fears. Our brains are designed to keep us safe, so even imaginary fears or problems are very real in our minds. When it's imaginary, you'll either want to fight or run. You'll take action out of fear. Maybe you'll start focusing on what you *should* make instead of what you *want* to make. Following the *should* is how you take the hard path.

If you want to take the path of least resistance, it's key to tap into and listen to your divine connection. You're always connected, but you're not always listening. Don't feel bad; we're all like this. When you get to check in and ask where the information is coming from, if you felt good when you received it, it's divine guidance. You can also actively practice connecting with your divine by asking for and receiving guidance.

I recommend adding the following practice to your daily routine. Here's how to connect, ask, and receive:

- Place your right hand on your heart and take a few deep breaths. Let yourself feel the breath in every cell of your being. Imagine tree roots coming up from Mother Earth to help ground you.

- Imagine a white light coming down from the ether. This is unconditional love. Let that light flow all the way from the top of your head down to your heart, then to your belly button, down to your toes. Let this light be unconditional love.

- Call in your inner being by saying in your mind, *Inner being, come down.* She will come down into the light and come to stand in front of you. When you see her, have a conversation with her and ask what you need to release in order to step into her shoes so you can be in alignment. It might be a belief, an idea, or some sort of trauma that needs healing. You can imagine you're wearing whatever she tells you as a coat. Imagine yourself taking off the coat. As you do, walk closer to your inner being.

- Repeat the process until you're in total and complete alignment with your inner being. When you're done, ask for guidance. For example, you might be stuck on what to say to your spouse about your business, or you might be looking for input on an investment offer you want to put out in the world. Whatever you do, ask and then let the answer come. You don't need to force it. If it doesn't come, it's not the right time. Try again later.

Once you feel connected, you'll feel really good. Bring that energy out into the world.

Remember, being a superhero in your personal and professional lives means you must be in alignment with your inner being. If you feel stuck or confused, chances are you just need to realign. This may happen daily, or more if you're out of practice, but you will get more efficient as you work this practice into your routine.

And, if all else fails, remember *Grey's Anatomy.* In one episode, Emilia Shepperd has a big surgery to remove another doctor's brain tumor. Of course, she's scared out of her mind, even though she's been preparing for months. A few minutes before the surgery, there's a scene where she and her resident are standing in superhero stance. According to Emilia, doing this before facing a problem is proven to provide a better outcome. After finding her courage, she steps into the operating room to do the most difficult surgery she's ever done, confident and connected to her inner truth and being.

By the way, the superhero stance is backed by research. It was found that a one-minute stance decreases your cortisol levels and allows you to increase your ability to take risk by 60 percent.

What would happen if you took your superhero stance out in the world? Try it today.

Principle #2
Believing Is a Choice—Choose It

Whatever the mind can conceive and believe, it can achieve.
—*Napoleon Hill*

When I was travelling in Zambia, I got the chance to do a gorge swing jump at the Zimbabwe–Zambia border. A swing jump is like a bungee jump except that you get into a kiddy swing before you jump off the cliff. Just like the bungee jump, you swing like a pendulum until you reach the bottom.

I stepped into the swing, and the safety crew tied ropes to me. They pulled on everything to make sure I was safe and told me to step on the ledge of the platform. *What am I doing?* I held my breath, closed my eyes, and leapt off the platform. A moment later, I had a full-blown wedgie as I swung from side to side.

Would you jump?

Some people would never sign up for the jump, let alone walk out onto the platform. Some make it to the edge but psych themselves out of actually jumping, their fear stopping them from having the experience. It takes a leap of faith (and courage) to jump.

We're talking about this here because deciding to live on purpose and growing your business is *full* of ledges and leaps of faith. You're constantly going outside of your comfort zone and free-falling into the abyss of the unknown. It's part of the game of entrepreneurship. You can't play if you don't jump.

One of the biggest leaps I took in my business was in early 2019. I spent $20,000 on Facebook ads and invited five thousand people to a group where I'd run a Facebook challenge. My goal was to enrol 100 women into my new, $1,000 signature program, Goddess Rising. The cart was open a total of six days, and I made a grand total of two sales. Yes, my group was interactive, and many people engaged, but almost no one bought. It was a hard blow, and I felt betrayed and like I had done something wrong.

In the weeks leading up to the challenge, I'd spent all my time and energy supporting the women in the challenge group. The 5,000-plus women in the challenge loved it. For the first time in a long time, I felt like I was serving, like I'd been taught by the gurus. I was up front about the fact that the doors to Goddess Rising would be opening during the challenge. The women in the challenge were excited about joining.

From a marketing standpoint, I did everything right—and then my cart opened, and everything fell apart. People took one look at the price and payment options and started telling me I'd tricked them into getting excited. Many of the women who previously testified to beautiful transformations during the challenge left nasty comments saying Goddess Rising was too expensive, telling me it wasn't for the average woman.

Every day, I did mindset work to shake off the pain of failing. I wrote down positive affirmations. I listened to Abraham-Hicks YouTube videos. Just in case you're unfamiliar with Abraham-Hicks, it's a set of teachings delivered by a set of entities called Abraham and interpreted by Esther Hicks on the Law of Attraction. They have also called themselves a group consciousness of non-physical beings. I like to think of Abraham as infinite intelligence.

Anyway, I reached out to my coach. I reframed what was happening and tried desperately to feel better. Unfortunately, I couldn't shake off this sinking feeling that my launch was a complete disaster. Seeing those comments even started to make me believe no one could actually afford it. I kept thinking no one would buy. In the end, only two people bought into the program, and I manifested my biggest fear.

The biggest lesson out of all of this: If you focus on fear and doubt instead of faith, you're screwed. You need to focus on what's possible, not what could go wrong. According to the Law of Attraction, what you focus on grows and gets returned to you. I was focused on fear, and my fears materialized. It was the only vibration going out. I believe if I had brought myself out of fear and back to faith *every day* in the program, the results would have been different.

Fear and doubt are not bad in and of themselves. Both feelings are your ego's way of trying to keep you safe. If you're in a tiger's cage, you want to respond to the fear. The problem is, most fear and doubt are based on made-up scenarios where you're not actually in any danger.

The truth is, you can't be sure of the outcome. People might question you, but then again, they might not. And even if they do question you, it may be from a place of curiosity or seeking to understand, not because they want to hurt you.

Nothing will zap your confidence and self-esteem like focusing on failures or lack of results. It's your job to believe in your dream and see through the process from beginning to end, regardless of the results you get.

You can't fake confidence

I have found that it's difficult and next to impossible to fake self-confidence when there is just too much self-doubt. Because the Law of Attraction returns to you results that match your vibration, if you're filled with doubt, and it's overpowering any feelings of confidence, the universe will return results that match the vibration of self-doubt. You won't get clients. Your launches will fail. You'll attract tire-kickers. It doesn't mean what you want doesn't exist; it just means you can't see the opportunities available to you. Even if you can force yourself to take action, you won't get the results you want.

That's what happened to me during the challenge. I went all out and hosted a Facebook challenge with 5,000 people who loved every minute—but then made only two sales for a total of $3,000 instead of the $100,000 I was hoping to make. You can't receive what you don't believe from the universe. More importantly, you can't wait for something to happen in order to believe. You have to choose to believe *now*.

How do you believe in something that hasn't happened yet?

When I went into my business, I had this daily practice of writing down my money and client goals, and I tried to tell myself they were possible. But honestly, I didn't think that they were. I was filled with doubt my money goals could and would happen.

Whenever I got clients, it felt like a miracle. It would do nothing for my confidence. At best, I believed it was a one-time thing and kept repeating the same limiting beliefs over and over again. *How do I trust? I'm filled with doubt. I don't know anything anymore.* The answer lies in understanding the universal Law of Polarity.

The Law of Polarity is the principle that everything has two poles: good and evil, love and hate, attraction and disconnection. Think of the North and South Poles on a globe or a battery with its negative and positive terminals. Everything in the universe has an opposite. This means that you can't have a dream without it existing out in the universe (it's the other side of the coin).

If you have a desire for money or clients, whatever it is, the desired thing is real and already in existence. You don't have to create the money, right? It already exists. There are plenty of opportunities for you to find your way to the money. And so, in the end, it's not about whether or not the desired thing is available, because in the Law of Polarity we know it is. It's just a matter of finding your way to what you desire.

The week I learned about the universal Law of Polarity, I wrote down the following: "I intend to manifest $10,000 this week. I know it's possible because the Law of Polarity states I wouldn't have this desire unless the money existed. I'll take advantage of every opportunity until it happens. Universe, show me the opportunities I can't see. I know they are out there."

The next morning, I received an email from an on-again/ off-again client telling me she was ready to go further with me. Four days later, I'd made my first $20,000 sale.

Is it that simple?

Though the first attempt worked, I tried again the following week, and I failed to manifest a single dime. Clearly, something was off. Did I truly believe I could manifest that much again? Part of me was truly resisting opportunity. Sometimes tasting success is enough to make you think you've reached your limit and won't have repeat success.

This is when I started to do the mindset work to clear the defiance and align with the knowing all goals are attainable. When you do this, you'll be in alignment with your inner self. This is a great time to start asking, "What can I do?" because you'll be open to the possibilities.

Rhonda's Story

When Rhonda came to me, she had a book was struggling with a lot of self-doubt. So I asked her to share her story. Here's what she wrote:

> I lost my boy, Jeremy, in a car accident when he was just 18. After he passed, I connected with him in the spirit world—anything to keep the connection alive. Over time, Jeremy sent me teachings, which I put in a book, *Jeremy Shares His Love from Above*. It helped me rise above my grief.
>
> The thing you need to know is that I had a lot of doubts as I went through the process. I wondered if I was channeling and interpreting properly. Yet there was something in my heart that said writing a book was the right thing

to do. It's weird, but I knew I had to get through it.

When I was just about to publish the book, I reached out to Nathalie for help. I knew that I needed to let go of the resistance and get out of my way. She likes to say I was in the driver's seat but had one foot on the gas and one foot on the brake. I struggled to trust myself, and working with Nathalie allowed me to let go of doubt and start believing in and trusting my own divine connection.

The trust that I found in myself as I worked with Nathalie lasted, too. It's like I've stepped into a whole new phase of my life, and I'm following my joy. No more trying to follow the *should*. I'm also much better at trusting the opportunities that are out there.

You have divine gifts. Let them come through you.

Rhonda

How do you clear your energy and get in alignment?

There are three steps for getting out of doubt and into unstoppable confidence. First, you must dump all of the thoughts in your head. Then, you must choose new beliefs. Finally, you must practice living at the vibration of what it is you want. Here's how you do this:

Step #1: Dump out your head

The objective here is to identify all the running negative thoughts keeping you in fear and doubt. When I do this exercise with clients, I find people don't want to identify the thoughts in their heads. They'll say something like, "I'm afraid I'm too expensive, but in my head I know my price is reasonable," or "I keep thinking I'm not good enough, but deep down I think I am."

Denying your negative thoughts just represses them and gives them more energy. If you want to get through them and lessen their power, you must identify, acknowledge, and release them. You do that by writing down the thoughts. Here's an example:

$6,000 in cash in next 3 days.

What I really believe right now:

- There's not enough time to get everything done.
- I'm not good enough to make it work.
- It's impossible.
- I don't have enough time to take sales calls.
- I've never had more than two or three clients a week, let alone a month.
- It's too expensive.
- No one has the money.
- There's no point.

Step #2: Choose new beliefs

Now that you have written down your negative beliefs, you want to choose new beliefs. You want to create thoughts that support your goal and belief system.

This is not about writing down a bunch of things you don't believe. The key to making this work is to find beliefs—usually more general, fact-based statements—that allow you to get into a state of believing. If you get stuck, ask yourself what you would need to believe for the goal to come to life? For example:

- It would feel good to receive $6,000 this week.

- The Law of Polarity says I wouldn't have a desire without its availability.
- There are lots of ways the money could come. It could come through business, or I could sell belongings, or I could borrow it. Maybe I could get a side job. I could increase my credit card limit or get a new one. I could get a credit line.
- There's plenty of time. The Universe is never late.
- There are lots of opportunities for me to receive $6,000 in cash this week.
- My inner being is showing me and guiding me along the way.
- I'm so excited to receive the next step.
- I'm really good at receiving divine downloads and acting.

Note that this is not about listing things you are going to do. It's about allowing the universe to show you there are existing opportunities. If you can come up with ten ways to receive it, consider that proof it's possible.

If you want to know more about how to choose new aligned beliefs, read *Ask and Given* by Esther and Gerry Hicks. It provides twenty-two processes for get into a better-feeling state.

Step #3: Practice the vibration

A lot of people think the Law of Attraction is, simply, that thoughts attract thoughts. In fact, that's not quite accurate. The truth is that like-vibration attracts like-vibration. It means if you practice the vibration of what you desire, the path to what you want will come. To do so, you must practice the *feeling* that you already have what you want.

Ask yourself, *What does it feel like to receive my goal?* Imagine yourself receiving $6,000. See yourself telling your friends of your win. What does it feel like? What are you doing? What beliefs do you have about yourself now that you've succeeded? How do you show up in the world differently? In your stance? Your mindset? Your business?

Here's an example of me feeling my goal:

> *I really love the abundance that flows through the universe. I love the people excited to join in and sign up. I love the exchanges between us and the connections made. When I look around and see the impact, I see myself helping them put even more abundance into the river. There's a ripple effect that I love. I love the satisfaction that comes from success, from living my purpose, and from*

> *connection. I love how easy it is to receive. I love*
> *how crazy abundant the universe is.*

Once I've envisioned this, I stop and feel it. I imagine a ray of light coming down from the ether. It comes through the top of my head, then moves down through my heart center, all the way to my feet, with the feeling of light and peace radiating through my entire body.

One last thought

Doing the above exercise isn't always sexy (or easy). It's not like creating a new offer or putting up a new funnel. It's more like brushing your teeth to avoid cavities. It's just something you have to do to get forward momentum in your business. Your doubts create your reality. If you don't bring your focus back to faith, you will get stuck and stay stuck in your business.

I know it would be easier if I promised you it worked on the first day or that this was an easy, quick change. My challenge to you? Commit to this for 30 days and see what happens. You might not reach your goal, but you'll be a whole lot closer by taking inspired action every day.

What would happen today if you chose to believe in your dream was possible?

Principle #3
Follow What Energizes You

> The simple way to figure out who you
> are and what you want is to start aligning
> yourself with things that energize you.
> —*Mel Robbins*

Ever since I can remember, I've wanted the freedom of owning an online business. The idea that you can live anywhere in the world was exciting to me, and still is, but how do you get clients online?

I started to cyberstalk a few well-known, talented business coaches, including Marie Forleo, Jenny Shih, Bill Baren, and Callan Rush. I signed up for every free resource they offered on how to grow a list, grow an online tribe, build a brand, and sell. It's through them that I learned that the best way to grow my business was to niche down and pick a problem to solve.

Apparently, healing work was not a problem I could solve for people.

The more I listened to these gurus, the less of a clue I had about the problem I solve. I decided, despite my confusion, that it was time to move, because otherwise my business wouldn't go anywhere, and I needed it to work so I could leave the IT world behind. I typed the words *niche coaching* into Google, and up popped Rhonda. I immediately booked a breakthrough call with her, and by the end of it, I handed her my credit card.

In exchange for $6,000, she would show me how to find and pick a niche and build my online presence. By the end of our six months together, I would have clients—or that was the plan. Excited, I dove right into her training, and I followed it to a T. After all, I wanted to be successful.

The first step was to pick a group of people I wanted to work with and decide on the problem. She had me list all the professions I could think of, from real-estate agents to project managers. The next step was to pick one.

I decided to build my new online business helping project managers find better projects for higher pay. Now that totally made sense, but there was one problem: my heart wasn't in it. It had nothing to do with the healing work I was passionate about.

I didn't tell her my heart wasn't in it or there was exactly zero passion in it. I ignored this feeling and kept pushing through the steps of her program. I built a website, wrote copy, and created a free online gift. When it came time to start promoting and telling people about my new business, I wanted to puke, and I just kept thinking, *I'd rather stick needles in my eyeballs than help project managers find better projects. What's wrong with me? Why can't I just go out and get clients? I did all this work. Is it possible I'm just scared? Just push through it, Nathalie!*

Now I know there are times when you just need to push through the resistance and get it done, but this wasn't one of them. It was completely out of alignment. It wasn't exciting. It wasn't me. If you're not excited about the service, offering, or product you're offering, you shouldn't do it. You didn't start this business to do something you hate.

So I did the unthinkable and ditched this newfound niche. I asked myself, *What do I actually want to do?*

Eventually, after some trial and error and asking myself the same question over and over, I finally decided to help entrepreneurs manifest a business and life they love. I stopped IT consulting and went into my business full time. It felt right.

What does this have to do with unlocking your potential?

If you're not excited about doing something, you're naturally going to look for reasons to stop, so save yourself some time: Anything that doesn't truly excite you needs to be dropped.

When you're following what energizes you, you naturally focus on your goal. You're effortlessly excited to figure out how to make it happen. When you're truly pumped about making it happen, challenges won't faze you, and you'll be willing to face your fears (they will come up).

When you're energized by something, you're in alignment. When you're in alignment, your light is strong. I believe people are craving this kind of connection. Your ideal clients are craving it. When they see it in you, they will reach out to you and get it done.

Alignment is your secret weapon

When I first started teaching Theta Healing, I was in complete alignment. I had made a very clear decision to teach. I knew that no matter what happened, I would figure out a way to enrol clients. The fact that I had no idea how to get clients never bothered me. I knew that the inner knowing was done. In that energy of pure vibration alignment, I had faith in my dream, the universe, and the unfolding. I knew I would figure it out.

In case you're wondering, all I did was post a crappy ad on Craigslist, and forty students showed up over the next eight months. It was easy. I thought getting clients was easy! I couldn't understand why people were struggling. Once I stopped being so excited about it, the same marketing yielded three students in a twelve-month period. Energy trumps marketing. If you're energy isn't in it, your marketing isn't going to work.

About your offers

It's not enough to be energized by your offers; your clients must also be energized by what you're offering. The best way to do this is to solve a problem you're excited about solving and one clients need resolved. With Wild, Happy &

Rich, I help women go from suffering with a soul-crushing career to living on purpose by helping them get unstoppable confidence.

Carola's Story

When Carola came to me, she was feeling a bit burned out. After I helped her reconnect to her divine guidance, she started to ask, "What's my purpose?" She looked into building affiliates. It was always based on the *should*.

The more she did the inner work, the more she came back to herself. She's a skilled healer and wants to do healing work. All of the busywork was just a distraction. Now she's started to take on her first clients.

What if your offer doesn't sell?

I've had plenty of flops, even when I was totally excited about those offers. You will too. There's a process of learning what works for you and what works for your tribe. The only way to do that is create an offer and put it out in the world to test it.

If it doesn't sell, it doesn't mean the offer is bad or it's too expensive. It might mean you haven't positioned it well. It might mean you haven't reached your tribe, or you haven't told enough people about it. If you're having doubts about your offer, do your mindset work and get in alignment with it (principle #5).

Once you fix your energy by getting into alignment, decide on your next best step. I highly recommend hiring a one-on-one business coach to check that your offer makes sense. If you do hire, make sure you're excited about working with those individuals and they with you. They will be able to guide you on the right path moving forward.

Whatever you do, don't give up too early. If you're struggling to believe, ask for a clear sign from the universe in the next seventy-two hours about your next step. The universe will deliver.

Jen's Story

When Jen came to see me she was really struggling to get momentum until she stopped following the guru's and started to follow her own inner wisdom. I asked Jen to share her experience. Here's what she wrote:

> When I discovered coaching, I knew I had to
> pursue it. When I niched down to help women
> recover from breakups with an emphasis on
> self-care, I started to do everything I could

to make my business work online. I took courses, created content, created a webinar, and even did breakthrough calls to enrol clients. Everything worked for a while, but I couldn't get any real momentum.

Working with Nathalie, I started to let go of what I *thought* I should do and I started to follow my truth. When I finally let go and started doing what was fun for me, talking about self-care and doing meditation, my classes filled up without me putting in effort. Working with Nathalie made it possible for me to choose what felt good to me.

If there's one tip I can give you, it's to get good at failing. Just pick yourself up, learn, and keep going. Failures are stepping stones, giving you the skills you need to fully live up to your potential.

Remember, it doesn't have to be so hard. Following your truth can be fun!

Get energized about your prices

How much should I charge for this offer? My time? You're going to hear a thousand different reasons, whys, and hows for determining what to charge your clients. It doesn't mean one is better than the other.

How much should you charge? First, make sure you're not undercharging. It doesn't matter what anyone else in your area is charging, nor does it matter what your teacher charges. You get to choose what feels good and fair for the work you're creating. If guilt or fear are causing you to undercharge (or hesitate to charge what you want), you need to clear your energy.

Imagine yourself charging three times as much for this offer. Feel the discomfort of it all. Send love to the discomfort, fear, and guilt—and then release it. Imagine receiving the money: how do you feel? How does it feel to earn money for doing what you love? Embrace the goodness and warmth of success. Once you can visualize yourself receiving it, go back to the original asking price and see if it feels fair or if another price feels more in alignment with your soul. By the time you finish this process, you should have a price you're excited about.

Check your energy when you're investing

A few years ago, I went to a Tony Robbins event in Montreal. One of the speakers who came before him was Phil Town, who teaches investment. I'd never heard of him before that day, but his story of how he went from raft guide to making it big in the stock market was truly inspiring. When he mentioned that retirement savings aren't growing fast enough, everyone in the room leaned in. He pitched the audience the chance to attend a three-day workshop in Montreal for $97. The crowd went wild, and so many people stood up to get their order form that they ran out. The energy he created was phenomenal.

I got up and ran toward the front of the room, along with half the audience. It's easy to get carried away by the excitement of it all, maybe even to purchase something you don't really need when others are eager to make a purchase. Before you hand over your credit card, ask yourself, *Is this something I really want to do? Will it get me closer to my goal?*

I've felt that kind of energy listening to webinars. I get supercharged by a presenter's story, solution, and offer. One guru who does this extremely well is Russel Brunson, the co-founder of Click Funnels.

If you begin to feel like you need an offer or won't succeed, take a moment and a step back. Breathe. Check in with yourself and ask the following:

- Is my heart truly excited about this offer?
- Is this the best next step for me?
- Am I truly excited about following this strategy?
- If the answer is no, why? Is it fear talking?

Don't overthink this exercise. Trust your heart. Doing this every time you make a decision will save you a ton of money and make the process so much more fun.

If you're still having doubt, ask the Universe to give you a very clear sign in the next 48 hours that doing this program is the right answer. Do this by writing down the following: *I demand that the Universe give me a clear sign this program is right for me in the next 48 hours.*

The sign will come, and you may like the answer. Follow through on what the sign is telling you. You never know. You might get a sign it's time for you to move forward in your business. You might get a sign it's time for you to let go of something to make room for the new. Whichever way the universe is telling you to go, that is your path.

The path to your desires is the path of joy

Follow the impulses that feel good.—Abraham-Hicks

Want life to be easier? Start trusting your divine connection and follow what energizes you, even if it doesn't make complete, rational sense. Usually, it won't.

Once, during a road trip across the country, I entered the United States at the Michigan border to get to Chicago by end of day. As I got closer to the I-94, my GPS told me to stay right. I intuitively felt this was wrong but questioned myself, because the GPS said otherwise. Of course, I followed the GPS, and all of a sudden, I ended up getting off in a busy city in the middle of a rush hour.

OMG. I knew better.

If you haven't done this with a GPS, I'm sure you've done it with a family member, friend, or perhaps a coach. You asked them what they thought you should do, and they were more than happy to advise. You followed their advice even though, in your heart, you knew it wasn't right for you, and you ended up hopelessly stuck. I nearly killed my business after my coach told me to raise my rates to $5,000.

Other people don't know better than you. They might know the right way for *them* and what *they* might do, but only *you* know what's right for *you*. It's time to trust yourself to follow your energy. You can't get it wrong.

Yes, it's scary. A lot of the women I work with struggle with trusting their energy. Yet we all need to remember we used to trust our intuitions much more. As kids, when we were excited about something, we went after it full blast. We never thought of the consequences of the action or of failing. We simply followed our desires. So why is this so hard for adults?

At some point, you got hurt and stopped trusting yourself. When you got blindsided by a guy you liked and got dumped; when you woke up one day and realized you'd jacked up your credit cards and made a complete mess of your finances; when you lacked the courage to leave your soul-crushing job to go do what you really wanted to do and ended up with depression; when you trusted someone who took advantage of that trust by abusing you; when you invested in coaches and programs that felt right and didn't get a return on an investment ... There are a million and one reasons to doubt yourself. It's OK to admit you don't trust your energy anymore. There's nothing wrong with you because of it, but now that you know better, you can and will benefit from doing something about it.

What happened after I got stuck in rush-hour traffic? After getting pissed at the GPS, I kept following it even though the decision felt off. I spent an hour going around in circles until I finally had enough and decided to follow the highway signs in front of me.

Get good at failing

There will be times when you follow your energy, make the best decision for yourself, and still fall flat on your face. It might come from a $20,000 launch like it did for me, or it might come when you ask a client for a sale and the client says no. There's no way to tell how the failures will come. The only thing you must know is that there will be bumps along the way. Failures will happen, and you should embrace them.

Reframe those failures. Find the good, keep learning, and move on. There are no mistakes. None of the steps you took were the wrong ones. I believe you needed to take those steps because you had something to learn.

Having a crazy amount of debt because of my business taught me I can survive failure, and it taught me how to get resourceful. Is that ideal? No. But anyone who has faced down less-than-perfect circumstances will tell you that finding the good inside of them is what helps you move forward.

Yes, I might have had fewer bills to repay, but I wouldn't be here writing this book without my failures. I wouldn't be living my purpose.

Each step, misstep, and reframe brought me closer to my goals. If you find the resiliency to keep moving forward, you'll learn there's gold in this journey. The path will reveal itself no matter how many failures you've had or how many mistakes you've made. And failing doesn't define you. You're still a divine human being. You're still perfect.

To get back into alignment after failure (or if you have remaining shame), you will need to make peace with your past. For example, staying angry over debt you incurred doesn't actually move you forward. Sure, it might keep you from repeating an old pattern, but it might also keep you trapped if you limit yourself based on a previous mistake. Everything you desire is outside the box, so you have no choice but to let go of what you perceive as failure.

Here's how to let go of a failure

To work through your negative beliefs and emotions, follow these steps:

- Take a few deep breaths. Once you're done, write the story. It's not about spelling, grammar, or form. Just

43

let the words—of what happened from beginning to end—come. Don't judge it; don't overthink it. Just write.

- Now, think about your feelings in relation to what happened. Then we'll analyze your emotional ties to the past. Finish the sentences "I feel ___" and "It means that ___." Don't judge the thoughts that are running through your head, just acknowledge them.

- Ask yourself: How strong is the negative energy you're feeling on a scale of 1 to 10 (1 is low, 10 is high)?

- Next, scan your body for the energy you identified. Determine where you feel it and how it makes you feel physically. Once you have it, send love to it. Imagine a ray of light coming from the ether down to the energy. You can repeat, "I love you. I forgive you. I'm sorry. Thank you." As you do so, you can let it go with more ease.

- Then determine how strong the negative energy you're feeling is on a scale of 1 to 10 (1 is low). If it's higher than 1, repeat the above process until you are certain you're at a 1 or a 0.

- Finally, when you can look at this with neutrality, ask yourself what you learned from it and how you want to be different moving forward. For example, you might have learned compassion, boundaries, forgiveness, and to ask more questions in the future.

There's always learning if you're looking to learn, and new information is a great way to let go of old hang-ups. Remember, letting go of the past doesn't mean you forget the experience or that the experience is OK, just that you no longer want the energy of that experience to hinder your present and future.

How to make the right decision for you

With so much information readily available in so many mediums, it can be overwhelming to know which step— whether simple or complicated—is the best or most appropriate for you. You don't have to create a complex marketing strategy to get clients. Instead, you have to follow the strategy that feels like the best place to put your energy.

If you want to be a guest on podcasts and invite people into a breakthrough call, do that.

If you feel called to create a webinar funnel, do that.

If you're inspired to sell from the webinar, do that.

If you're inspired to sell from a breakthrough call, don't let anything stop you.

Don't feel guilty about doing what you love. It's the goal, isn't it? As Abraham-Hicks says, "As long as you are letting your joy be your guiding light, you can always stay in balance."

How to get energized about your goals

- *Write down your goals and action steps on a piece of paper.* As you connect with your heart, finish the sentence "I feel ___." Keep repeating it until you've identified everything you feel. Once you're done with that, do the same with this prompt: "My mind says that ___." Don't hold back.

- *Feel the energy and send love to it.* The best way to do this is to imagine the heavy energy coming out of your heart into a balloon in front of you. Give the balloon a color. Connect to it. Once it's all done, imagine a ray of light coming down from the ether (unconditional love) and showering the balloon with unconditional love until it releases.

- *Choose your beliefs.* What do you want to believe about this goal? Write down your new beliefs supporting you in this manifestation. *Why am I excited about this goal? What do I believe to be true?* For example, "It would be nice to help so many people. I am capable. I've come a long way, and I'll figure this out. I really love knowing the universe is showing me the way." The key here is to make these statements general enough that you believe them.

- ***Get clear on your decision.*** If it's a new goal, is this something you want? If it's not, what action should you do? I learned these questions from David Neagle, and I've adapted them here. Ask yourself:

  o Is this something my heart really wants to do?
  o Is this something that excites me?
  o Am I doing this out of fear? If so, would I still make this decision without the fear?
  o Is the action/goal/strategy in alignment with the time frame?

- Once you've decided and it feels good, get into action. The faster you do, the faster you get results or not, and you get to move forward.

What would happen if you got clear about your goal and started to follow what energized you every day for 30 days? Curious? Do it.

Principle #4
Take the Wheel

> You might well remember that nothing
> can bring you success but yourself.
> —*Napoleon Hill.*

You were born to make an impact in the world, but it's not enough to *want* to make an impact or *want* to build a business to change lives. You must commit and go all in. In other words, you have to get into the driver's seat and start.

Yes, a good number of entrepreneurs work their butts off and dog everything they can to move their business forward, for months and even years, without ever getting a single client. It seems like they are in the driver's seat, but they are not. They aren't actually navigating the terrain or changing their routes when applicable. They're on autopilot in the same ineffective routine, getting busy instead of getting better.

If you're spending all your time building content, building websites, or scrolling Facebook feeds and you're not getting clients, you're hiding behind busywork. It makes you feel accomplished, but ultimately, it's an empty effort keeping you playing small and broke.

What does it mean to get into the driver's seat? You know where you want to go, and you're excited about going there. Even though you may not know how to get there, you're 100 percent committed to figuring it out. You have unstoppable confidence in your ability to get an answer. You check in with yourself and see what you really want and need before making decisions. Ultimately, you're acting, not on autopilot, to move the needle in your business. When you hit a roadblock, you pick yourself back up and keep going.

By the way, things change quickly in business, so just because you were in command of your decisions two weeks ago doesn't mean you always will be. It's important to reassess your effectiveness often, to make sure you don't get sidetracked by busywork.

How you get into the driver's seat for your business

Stop waiting for the right time, to be ready, or to figure out the *how*. There is no right time to start putting yourself out there, telling people what you want, and asking for the sale. You're never readier than right now. Seriously, you don't have to take another training, finish your website, create loads of content, or build a massive following on social media. The *how* will be revealed as you take action, so stop trying to figure it all out. Whatever plan you make can change and evolve. Just take the next best step.

If you're thinking you have to do XYZ before you create and sell the offer you're truly excited about (retreat, group program, etc.), stop waiting. That excitement is your sign it's time for you to get out there or to charge what truly energizes you. Waiting for the right time is just fear. The fastest way through fear is action.

If you're terrified, that means it's time to release the power fear has on you so you can take action even if you're afraid. Here's how you take your power back over the fear:

- **Ask *What's the worst that can happen if I do this?*** Don't say *nothing*. There's a reason you're letting fear get in the way, and it's time to clear it. It doesn't matter if the fear is real or just a figment of your imagination. Your feelings can't really tell the difference. For example: *I'm afraid people will think I'm fat. Or that I don't know what I'm talking about.*

- Ask ***What happens to me then?*** How would you feel? What does it mean? Keep asking until you find you can't go any further. For example: *I'll be judged for being heavy, so I'll feel ashamed. I'm not good enough to help myself, let alone others. I'm a fraud.*
- Ask ***What am I really afraid of?*** For example: *I'm afraid I am a fraud.*
- **Clear the energy**. Feel the energy of *I'm a fraud* by repeating it out loud. Let the negative emotions or discomfort come up to the surface. Give your feelings space to breathe. Imagine them becoming a cloud around you. Put your hand on your heart and send love to these emotions. You can even say *I love you* over and over again until the energy dissipates. You'll know your done when you can say *I'm afraid I am a fraud* without the charge.

Repeat the process until you can see yourself taking the action you want with success. It's quick and easy.

Don't just say you're all in, commit 100 percent. Feel it in your bones. Know in your heart you will reach your destination. Have faith in your ability to figure it out.

There is no try. Only do or do not.—*Yoda*

The biggest mistake people make here, and I make it all the time, is to *try* to do something. The truth is, when someone says, "We'll see how it goes" or "I'll try it and see," what they're really saying is that they don't want to commit to either success or failure because they don't fully believe they can do it. That's like sitting on the fence. Sometimes you'll follow through, but mostly you'll just watch like a pigeon and never actually do anything.

Take inspired action

Let's begin to inch you forward to move the needle on your business. You need to know your path is unique to you and is not linear. Any path I have shared with you isn't the only one. You might not want to create offers; you might want to simply offer sessions by the hour. I know healers and coaches who do really well with that model. At the end of the day, follow what brings you joy.

Sometimes the right path will be filled with resistance. It's why some people will tell you to lean into the resistance (or fear) and do it anyway.

Kristi's Story

That's exactly what happened to Kristi Dear, a mom of three and a success and mindset coach. She'd been slowly growing her business, and it hadn't yet taken off in the way she wanted when she decided to invest in a network marketing company—even though she didn't believe she could make it then.

If other people are doing it, why not me? Kristi thought.

With that change in mindset, she leaned into it and soon found herself with a seven-figure business in network marketing. Not only that, but she was now doing more coaching and speaking then she ever had before. The opportunities are all around you, but you have to choose them.

Listen, everyone on the planet is a judgement-making machine. Every time you do anything, you're being judged. Give up trying to control it. Trust yourself. Follow your next best step and do what needs to be done. Only then will you get to the next step and, eventually, your goal.

If you're not sure what to do, ask the Universe for a clear sign about your next steps. When you ask, the universe provides.

Want a sign from the universe? Do this:

- Get clear on the question you're asking the Universe and write the Universe, asking to receive a clear sign within a desired amount of time (be specific).

- If you still feel like you're not getting a sign, look around you and find something attention-grabbing. It might be a broom, a message board, a chair, or even a tree if you're outside. Ask, *If I was truly connected right now, what would it be telling me about this current situation?* You'll start to see an image or get a sensation. You might visualize the broom sweeping, telling you to let go, or you might see yourself cleaning a window, telling you that you need to get clarity. Or you might see a car zoom by and realize that it's time to step on the gas.

It shouldn't take long to get a sign. Once you have it, take the wheel and act. Only then will you discover the next step.

Get More Visible ...

One of the biggest things stopping people from getting visible is that they don't know what to do or say. It doesn't matter if you're a total newbie or have been in business for a few years, this is one area where people get afraid of showing up.

You need to know it's normal to be afraid of being seen. We crave the spotlight, but we aren't sure what to do when we're being ourselves and truly being seen. It's vulnerable and intimidating. If someone has a bothersome opinion of you, it's because you have that opinion of yourself.

When you're feeling judged, do this:

- Write down how and why you're being judged.
- Once you have it, finish the sentences: "I feel ___" and "It means that ___." These are all the thoughts of people running amok in your head. It's another way of dumping your head. Don't be embarrassed by these thoughts, just write them out.
- Ask yourself, *How strong is the negative energy I'm feeling on a scale of 1–10?*
- Now scan your body for this energy. Once you identify it, send love to it. Imagine a ray of light coming down from the ether to the energy. You can repeat *I love you, I forgive you, I'm sorry, thank you* as you do so you can let it go with more ease.
- Then, check back in: How strong is the negative energy you're feeling on a scale of 1–10? If your answer is higher than 1, repeat the above process until you're finally at a 1 or a 0.

- Now that you can look at this with neutrality, ask yourself what you want to believe. Do you want to sacrifice your truth for their opinion? Take your power back and decide what you choose to believe.

Finding your unique voice is a must

Finding your voice takes time, and the only way it can happen is for you to start putting yourself out there, using your voice. Russel Brunson, the cofounder of Click Funnels, is comfortable on video, doing talks, and going on podcasts. Sometimes it seems like he's invaded my newsfeed. But he didn't start that way. He often shares the story of how he sweated his way through his first webinar in a very monotone voice. He got better with practice.

Some people might start out with more natural confidence or skill, but everyone struggles. When I started out, I was trying to be perfect and figure out my voice before I used it. Except the only way to figure out your voice *is* to use it. Only through practice will you find your confidence. In the meantime, trust yourself to get through and figure it out. That's what unstoppable confidence is.

I want to challenge you to start by creating a piece of content every day for a hundred days. Choose a medium you like and commit to it. If you like podcasts, do podcasts. If you like Instagram, do Instagram. If you like Facebook, do Facebook. If you like writing, write a blog post every day. Follow what energizes you. Have fun with this process. Allow yourself the chance to fail. More than anything, believe it's the right path for *you*.

It's not enough to be energized by possibilities. You also have to get into the driver's seat and get started.

One last thought

I spent two years scrolling newsfeeds without ever posting. I was scared to interact. I was afraid to be seen. I was afraid to be judged. I often asked myself, *What's wrong with me? Why can't I get clients?* and believed ridiculous things like *I'm not ready.* I wasn't in the driver's seat. I was hiding behind the busywork. It wasn't until my very expensive business coach told me to start posting every day that I finally started. To my surprise, it became super-fun, and I had zero problem engaging.

I'm guessing you know what to do next in your business, but you're stalling. What would happen if you decided to get in the driver's seat and drive? Go. It's time. The world needs you.

Principle #5
Practice Alignment

> Universal Lesson: we are not responsible for
> what our eyes are seeing. We are responsible
> for how we perceive what we are seeing.
> —*Gabrielle Bernstein*

In October of 2016, I was working my butt off. I'd been steadily trying entrepreneurship for 18 months, and my business still wasn't growing. In fact, it seemed to be going backward. I'd put on 30 pounds since I started and spent a lot of time sitting on my couch with my cat, trying to pretend I was OK.

But I wasn't OK. I was on the verge of tears, and my cat was my only witness.

Should I quit? This is what I was thinking as I watched yet another training on how to succeed as a coach. The speaker told the story of the day she sat on her couch, on the verge of tears, with only her dog by her side. "If I'm going to survive," she said, "I'm going to have to figure out my thoughts."

It felt like she had looked inside my body, saw my heart, and whispered hope to it. That was the moment I knew I needed to manage my thoughts. My constant worry about what I was doing wrong was killing my business. It's also when I knew healing wasn't enough: it was an important step, but mindset and thought work required constant effort, too.

Admitting this was hard, because I was embarrassed I didn't understand mindset. You see, I'd spent years helping clients heal their beliefs and manage mindset (which is exactly what I wasn't doing for myself). I gave them exercises to do, helping them release resistance and get in alignment. They found their voices and the courage to follow their hearts, and often manifested incredible opportunities, yet I couldn't do it for myself. More than that, I didn't understand why I sometimes completed these exercises and manifested money like crazy and other times I was just broke and stuck.

Is there a secret to mindset work?

I started reading and searching for answers. My biggest breakthrough came when I finally realized mindset work and thought management are about being the person you need to create the life and business you want. It's about thinking like your ideal self. It's about being you at the core and allowing yourself to be you in your greatness. It's about being in alignment with your inner being. It's the part of you that believes your desires are already done. It's the part of you that enjoys the process and trusts the unfolding: the part of you that delivers.

The reason mindset exercises don't always work is that you're failing to get in alignment. Don't fake your way to success; become the version of *you* who is ready for success. Choose to align your thoughts and your actions with your inner being. While some people call it *mindset work*, I call it *alignment work* because that's the true goal of mindset work. It is not something you do for five minutes and you're done for life. It's something you practice every day. By that, I mean the practice of clearing your energy and getting back into alignment. You do the best you can on any single day, and you come back to it when you've steered off course.

Sarah's Story

When Sarah, a chiropractor, reached out to me, she was already doing pretty well in her business but wanted to increase her revenue to $20,000 a month. Considering she had the processes in place to attract clients, it was now a matter of energy. She understood the Law of Attraction but didn't understand why she couldn't maintain her momentum. Her success was like one step forward, one step back. Together we worked to set new goals and clear her energy, and she implemented a mindset practice that every time, her goals would be reached.

Sarah's message to you is, "You already know how powerful thoughts are, you have the basis to benefit from the work Nathalie does. You just have to show up and listen and have faith that your mind will crack open enough to let her do the work."

How do you know if you're in alignment?

If you feel good about your goal, you're in alignment. If not, you're not in alignment; you have resistance that needs to be cleared. Alignment occurs when you're truly feeling good about your desire. It's about believing in the desire even if you can't control it and even if you don't know how to achieve it. It's about choosing to believe your desire is already done. When you're in alignment, you can tap into your divine guidance and resourcefulness.

Before you go beating yourself up for thinking negative thoughts, know that it's normal. It's your ego protecting you from going outside of your comfort zone. There was a time when it saved you from lions. In this day and age, it's helping you pay attention. I believe these thoughts are a sign that you're growing. Not having any fear or negative beliefs would mean you're not going out of your comfort zone. You won't find success by playing it small or safe.

You can't control your thoughts, but you do get to choose whether you let them nest in your mind for weeks on end. You get to choose new thoughts that support your success (and evict the old, limiting beliefs).

How do you clear your energy and get in alignment?

If you google *mindset practices*, you'll get a bazillion results about how to do mindset work and how to get into alignment. Most of these exercises and examples are perfectly fine ways to do the work, but everything won't work for every person. You have to find the right tool for you.

No matter what you're doing, you're not going to always be in alignment. You're not always going to live in a constant state of joy. You're also going to experience struggles, growth, and pain because you are human. It's all part of the journey of life. No matter how much joy you have right now, life will always cause you to stretch. You will get out of alignment. The secret is to practice alignment on a regular basis.

Imagine you're a candle. When you're in alignment, you're shining bright. When you're not, your light dims to a point where it's barely burning. Practicing alignment turns your fire back up for the world to see and builds your unstoppable confidence.

> *Things don't have to be so hard, they can be fun.—Jen Amabile, client.*

If you're finding you're always starting new strategies—getting some results but never getting real longstanding results—it's because of what you believe or what you're not putting into practice. In my case, as long as I chased success and didn't actually get it, I could safely engage in the struggle. I felt accomplished because of my effort, but I didn't have to face the fear of actually stepping into my power and living my best life. I was in love with the cycle, and maybe you are too. I did healing work around it, which helped, but it was not until I started practicing alignment that the ease and flow started to come. Clients started to show up.

Here's how to practice alignment daily: Start your day with the following alignment practice. Make it non-negotiable. It doesn't matter if you don't feel like doing it, you can't skip it. It's just like brushing your teeth. If you skip, you'll feel icky.

Step #1: Align with your divine connection

- Put your right hand on your heart and take a few deep breaths.
- Imagine a ray of light coming down from the ether showering you with unconditional love. Enjoy the feel of it. With every exhale, let go of any tension you may be feeling. You have nowhere to be but right here, right now. Give thanks for three things in your life you're grateful for. These can be present, past, or future.

Step #2: Get energized

- Write down how you're feeling about two or three of your goals. *What I am feeling? What do I really believe?* For example: *I believe it's impossible* or *I'm struggling. It's really hard.* Or maybe something more positive like *It's going well. It's already done.*
- On a scale of 1 to 10, how much do you believe and know your desire can be achieved? What beliefs do

you have to release to believe fully and to know that it's true?

- Cross out each of your negative beliefs. Tell yourself, *My mind says I'm not good enough, but I am a spark of God, and I choose to believe I'm divine. I choose to believe this desire is done. After all, it's what the Law of Polarity teaches me. There are plenty of opportunities, and I'm ready to see them. I also choose to believe I have everything I need to succeed.* Feel free to adapt this to the beliefs you want to create.

Step #3: Feel it

What does it feel like to receive your desire? Spend a few moments feeling it, really anchoring it in every part of your being.

Step #4: Get into the driver's seat

- Set your intention for the day. Take out your journal and write out how you want your day to go. How do you want to feel as you go about your day? Who do you want to be? What do you believe today? If you want to go deeper here and have the best day ever, journal your day as if it was already done. Scripting, as it's called, really works.

- What's the next best step? Make sure you're taking actions to further your goals and further energize you.

Step #5: Go take action

If you're not getting the sales you want, the clients you want, or the love you want, it's time to stop what you're doing and do the alignment practice. If you're feeling like crap or you feel like quitting, stop everything and get to work on your mindset. You might have to do it once a day or 10 times a day, but it's the most important piece for finding your success.

Worrying about money is *not* practicing alignment, and it will keep you stuck

When I stopped getting a regular paycheck, I started worrying about money. Rationally, I knew it was crazy. I had access to plenty of money via credit lines and even my retirement savings. Despite this, I was always scared of running out. I even worried that when I made money in my business something would happen, like God would turn off the tap.

Ironically, it's only when I was almost broke again and I couldn't pay my mortgage that I finally surrendered and started trusting that the universe had my back. I started practicing the feeling of securing and knowing that all is well.

If you want to be abundant, you need to stop worrying about money. You need to find a way to be satisfied with what you've got. That's true whether you've got a lot or not enough.

There are some wonderful healers and coaches out there who deal with money blocks. It's well worth the investment, if you think this would benefit you. When you search for one, make sure these people have wealth themselves or a very good track record of helping other people make money. If they are broke, they shouldn't be helping you with money. One of my favorite books around this is *Tapping into Wealth* by Margaret Lynch. You can grab a copy off Amazon.

It might sound woo-woo to clear your money blocks, but I've worked with hundreds of clients around money, and every single time, I get blown away by how powerful this can be.

Kay's Story

My client Kay shares this account of how it happened for her:

> I'd just finished school and started my business
> as a music therapist. When I met Nathalie,
> money felt heavy, and it felt like my mountain
> of school debt was a life sentence. I wouldn't
> take another training or a trip. I was rather
> discouraged. After having a healing session
> with Nathalie to clear my energy around
> money, I had enough to take a trip, invest
> in training, and upgrade my apartment. The
> funny part is, the money was there all along,
> but it's like I'd kept the door closed.

Clearing your energy is one thing, but you'll also need to
stop worrying about money and find a place of satisfaction
with your current life. When you reach this state, you'll get
in alignment with your inner being. Like Kay, you will see
the opportunities available to you. You might notice there's
available money in your savings account to invest, or a client
might call you out of the blue. Or you'll get more resourceful.

Clearing your energy is the secret to getting real momentum in your business

Here a few ways to clear your energy:

- ***Do the dump your head exercise***, but do it around money and find a place of worry. When you're done, write down five or ten reasons you really love money. Make sure these statements don't focus on what you're lacking. They should feel good.
    - o I love the energy of money.
    - o I love knowing the money I desire is out in the Universe.
    - o I love that my inner being knows the way.
    - o I love the ripple effects money has in the world.
    - o I love getting paid well for the work I do.
- ***Stop tolerating money worry.*** Every time you notice yourself worrying about money, pivot and say, "Won't it be nice when there's plenty of money?" This works because it shifts your focus away from what's not working. This takes practice. You might have to do it once a day or 50 times, and every day will be different. Redirect your thoughts every time a money concern pops up, no matter how often it happens.

- ***Get resourceful.*** Make a list of at least 30 ways to bring in new money. When you get stuck, keep going. This will allow you to see money can come in from different sources. It doesn't have to come from your business; it could come from anywhere.
- ***Follow the energy.*** Which action would bring you joy? Go do that.

If you haven't yet, make sure to grab the Reset and Magnetize Ritual from my website, http://www.nathalieguerin.com/.

It's time to get in alignment with sales

I was shocked the first time I was paid for a psychic reading. I took the money and put it in my lap, but it was all I could do not to jump out of my seat. It was the first time in 18 years I'd made money outside of corporate, and it represented possibility.

I can do this.

My first client gave me the courage to go out and get another. Then, I raised my rates, and that made me insecure. Instead of allowing clients to pay me, I would give money back to them. I felt guilty for taking money. When I started creating packages with premium pricing, I would break and lower my rate.

I had zero confidence and hated asking for sales. I always had this feeling in the pit of my stomach that I was doing something wrong. Sure, I'd do energy work, and it would work for a while. But eventually, that feeling would return.

If you aren't confident about sales, you're going to struggle and, eventually, go out of business. Consider the following keys to overcoming that feeling of insecurity.

Key #1: Stop thinking you have to make the sale

Making sales isn't about putting pressure on the other person to buy from you. It's about making an opportunity that person will want to say *hell yes* to. That's a win-win. The best part? Once I realized this was about what the *client* wanted, I didn't feel pressured to make a sale. I could really be present for the person in front of me. And if that person didn't feel like someone who would benefit from what I offered, it felt OK to say, "This isn't a good fit for me right now." Lesson? You don't have to work with everyone.

Key #2: Stop trying to control the outcome; let people choose

I was hell-bent on making sure potential clients made the right decision for themselves. I didn't want to pressure them or lose money in the process. I really wanted other people to say yes, but I also didn't want to manipulate them. I'd been there before, and it wasn't fun. I didn't want people to invest and then later regret it. So I stopped trying to control the outcome and was confident that the right people who saw my offering's value would commit. Those were the people I wanted, not the ones I had to chase down or convince.

Secondly, even if they said no, it might not have anything to do with me. Not everyone has the money, and that's OK. Some people aren't ready to leap into it. Nobody's *no* makes me a failure.

Key #3: Stop charging based on what everyone else is charging

When your coach tells you to jack up your price to $5,000 because you're worth it, stop. Get back to your truth. Do the energy work. If you're not at peace, don't upgrade. If you're undercharging, do the energy work and start charging more. The key to getting into alignment with your price is making sure the transformation is valuable.

Get into alignment before a sales call so you can go into it with confidence. If you haven't yet, download the

Unstoppable Confidence pack from my website, http://www.nathalieguerin.com/.

Stop trying to get in alignment by yourself

It doesn't matter if you're the best healer or the best mindset coach in the world and help thousands with your skills. You don't have the ability to see your blind spots. It's easy to hide from your stuff and stay stuck in the pit of despair. The worst part is that not dealing with our mindset makes us feel like frauds.

Hire a transformational coach who will help you change your inner game. Find a healer and/or coach who believes in the power of the mind, understands mindset, and is able to guide you back to *you*. You will still need to do work on your own time, outside of what they ask you to do (read: mindset practice).

If you want my help, I invite you to join me for a complimentary breakthrough call. This is a call where you and I are going to figure out what's going on with your inner being and the best path forward to creating the life and business you want. If I can help you, I'll let you know how. If I can't, I'll let you know that too. Go here to http://www.nathalieguerin.com and follow the instructions to sign up.

I hate to say this, but some coaches are just out to tell people what to do. When you come across one, take back your power and walk away. Find someone who believes in you and truly supports you. You should feel this in your gut.

Don't let failures keep you out of alignment

As an entrepreneur, you will hit some pretty big speed bumps. You will invest in programs and strategies that don't get you the results you want. You will ask for the sale and get rejected. When you're failing and you're struggling, your job is to learn from it, get back into alignment, and keep going. If you're struggling to let go of past failures, do this:

- Write down a list of all the failures you've had that bother you or you still hold on to.
- Take a few deep breaths and connect with your heart. For each item on the list, connect with the energy and repeat the Ho'oponopono prayer, "I love you. I forgive you. I'm sorry. Thank you. I forgive me." Repeat it until you feel the energy release. It doesn't erase the experience, but it takes the energetic charge out of it. This will allow you to see more clearly and move forward.
- Call in your inner being by saying in your mind, *Inner being, come down.* She will come down into the

light and come to stand in front of you. When you see her, have a conversation with her and ask what you need to release in order to step into her shoes so you can be in alignment. It might be a belief, an idea, or some sort of trauma that needs healing. You can imagine you're wearing whatever she tells you as a coat. Imagine yourself taking off the coat. As you do, walk closer to your inner being.

- Repeat the process until you're in total and complete alignment with your inner being. When you're done, ask for guidance. For example, you might be stuck on what to say to your spouse about your business, or you might be looking for input on an investment offer you want to put out in the world. Whatever you do, ask and then let the answer come. You don't need to force it. If it doesn't come, it's not the right time. Try again later.

By the way, this is the perfect daily mindset routine.

One last note

Make mindset and alignment work non-negotiable. It's just something you have to do every day: no questions or excuses. It should be no different from any other part of your daily self-care routine. When you forget or just get lazy (it happens to me too), recommit and get back to it. You don't have to punish or shame yourself or do some crazy ritual for forgetting. It's more important to get back to it.

Want to know what's possible? Do the daily alignment practice every day for 30 days. Better yet, download your guided daily alignment practice for extra support. Go to my website, http://www.nathalieguerin.com/, for all the details.

ABOUT THE AUTHOR

Nathalie Guerin is a speaker, author, healer, and spiritual empowerment coach. For the last 10 years, she has helped hundreds of women rise into purpose, passion, and happiness. She is the creator of the Six-Figure Studio and Wild & Happy. The Six-Figure Studio is designed to help female entrepreneurs unblock their money blocks. She created Wild & Happy to help women break free from depression and create a life on purpose.

Nathalie Guerin holds a bachelor's degree in mathematics with a major in computer science. She spent 18 years doing everything from programming to project management. She specialized in process re-engineering and fixing troubled projects. She left the IT world six years ago to pursue her dream of entrepreneurship and start an online business. She has helped clients unleash their greatness, break free from their past, and find the courage to create a life on purpose. There's nothing better to her than seeing her clients expand into the people they need to be in order to create the result they want.

Her passion lies in helping people create/be/do/have their desires by using the laws of the Universe. She's been fascinated with this ever since she discovered just how powerful the Law of Attraction is and what's possible when you let go and let the universe guide you. All her life, she has been unstoppable in the pursuit of her dreams. She is the published author of *The Promise*, a book to help people through depression and the loss of suicide.

Nathalie Guerin is currently living in Montreal, Quebec. She loves to travel and spend time outdoors. Want to stay in touch? Grab the *free* Reset and Magnetize Ritual from her website, http://www.nathalieguerin.com/.

Printed in the United States
by Baker & Taylor Publisher Services